WISDOM

of

SLOTHS

A Firefly Book

Published by Firefly Books Ltd. 2024
Copyright © 2017 Moseley Road Inc.

All rights reserved. No part of this publication may be reproduced,
stored in a retrieval system, or transmitted in any form or by any means,
electronic, mechanical, photocopying, recording or otherwise, without the
prior written permission of the Publisher.

First printing

Library of Congress Control Number: 2023949121

Library and Archives Canada Cataloguing in Publication

Title: Wisdom of sloths / compiled by Lisa Purcell.
Names: Purcell, Lisa (Editor), compiler.
Identifiers: Canadiana 20230572812 | ISBN 9780228105022 (hardcover)
Subjects: LCSH: Quotations, English. | LCSH: Sleep—Quotations,
    maxims, etc. | LCSH: Laziness—Quotations, maxims, etc. | LCGFT:
    Quotations.
Classification: LCC PN6081 .P87 2024 | DDC 080—dc23

Published in the United States by   Published in Canada by
Firefly Books (U.S.) Inc.   Firefly Books Ltd.
P.O. Box 1338, Ellicott Station   50 Staples Avenue, Unit 1
Buffalo, New York 14205   Richmond Hill, Ontario L4B 0A7

Moseley Road Inc.
International Rights and Packaging
22 Knollwood Avenue
Elmsford, NY 10523
www.moseleyroad.com

President: Sean Moore
Project editorial and art director: Lisa Purcell
Photo research: Grace Moore

Printed in China | E

WISDOM

of

SLOTHS

Compiled by
Lisa Purcell

FIREFLY BOOKS

"*Ambition* is a **poor excuse**

for *not* having **sense**

enough to be **lazy.**

~ Milan Kundera

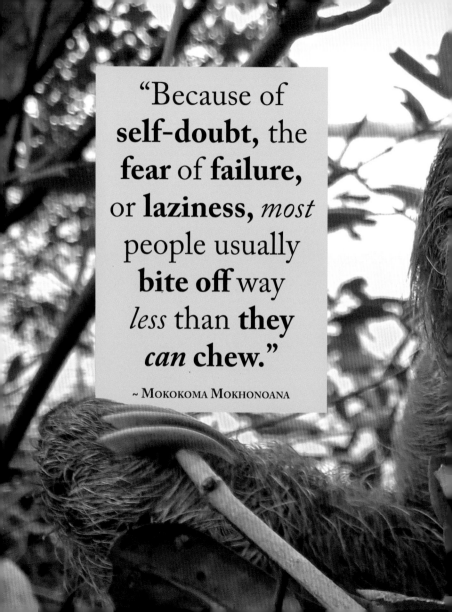

"Because of **self-doubt,** the **fear** of **failure,** or **laziness,** *most* people usually **bite off** way *less* than **they** *can* **chew.**"

~ Mokokoma Mokhonoana

"When the going gets tough,

the tough take a nap.

~Tom Hodgkinson

"If you **bungle** *raising* your **children,** I don't think **whatever** **else you** **do** *matters* *very much."*

~ Jacqueline Kennedy

"I've got **nothing** to do *today* but **smile.**"

~ PAUL SIMON

"It is **better** to **fail** in *originality* than to **succeed** in *imitation.*"

~ HERMAN MELVILLE

"Just *try* new things.

Don't be **afraid.**
Step out of your
comfort zones

and *soar,* all right?"

~ MICHELLE OBAMA

"*What* a **large volume**
of **adventures** may be
grasped within the
span of his **little life** by
he who **interests** his
heart in *everything.*"

~ Laurence Sterne

"The *best* way to make **children** *good* is to **make** **them** *happy.*"

~ OSCAR WILDE

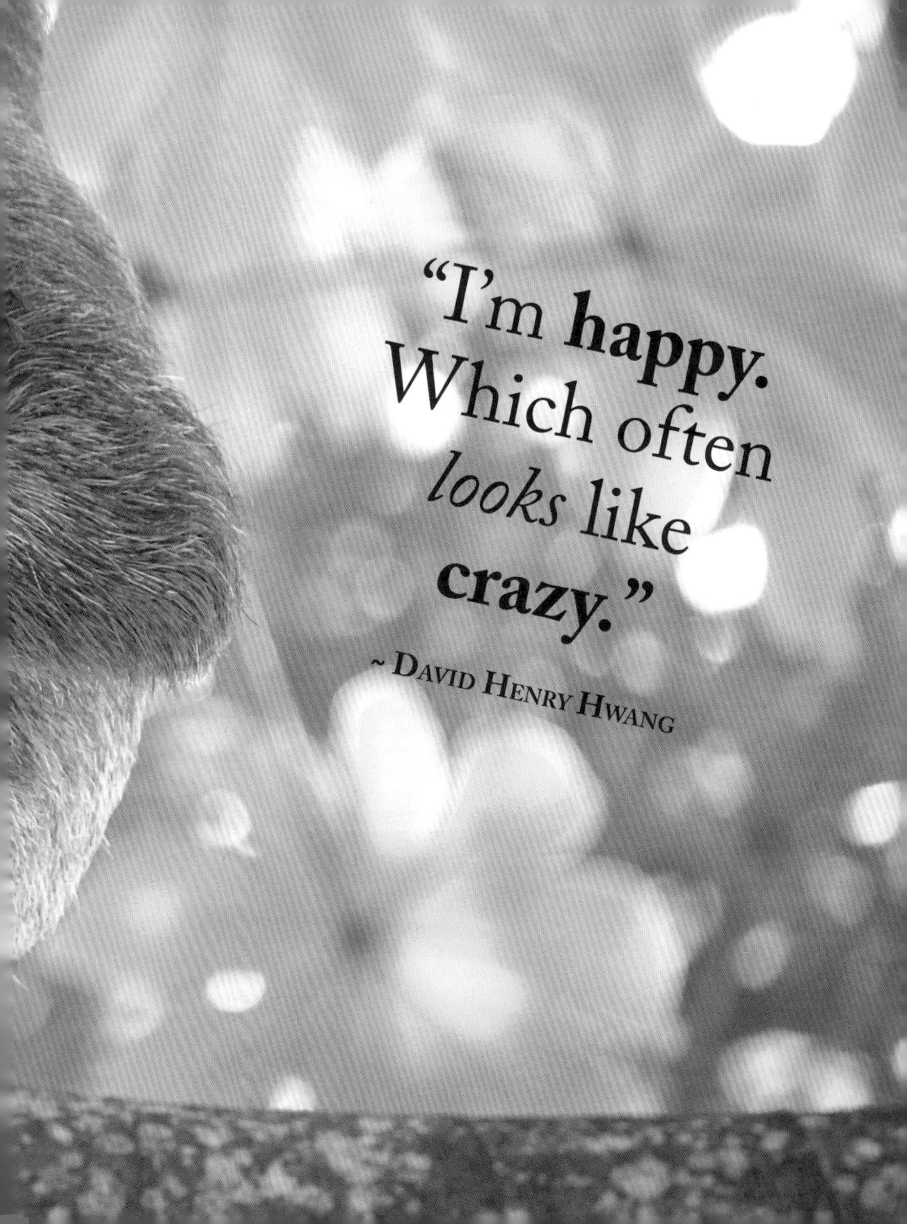

"I'm **happy.**
Which often
looks like
crazy."

~ DAVID HENRY HWANG

"I *must* **learn** to be **content** with **being** *happier* than I **deserve.**"

~ JANE AUSTEN

"Isn't it *nice* to think that **tomorrow** is a *new* **day** with **no mistakes** in it *yet?*"

~ L. M. Montgomery

"There *was* **another life** that I *might* have had, but I am having **this one.**"

~ KAZUO ISHIGURO

"*Sometimes* you **wake up.** *Sometimes* the **fall** kills you. And *sometimes,* **when** you **fall,** you **fly.**"

~ NEIL GAIMAN

"Fall seven times,

stand up *eight.*"

~ JAPANESE PROVERB

"**Imperfection** is **beauty,** **madness** is **genius** *and* it's better to be **absolutely** *ridiculous* than **absolutely** *boring.*"

~ Marilyn Monroe

'If you're **young** *and* **talented,**

it's like you have **wings.** "

~ HARUKI MURAKAMI

"Do *your* thing

and

don't

care if

they

like it."

~ TINA FEY

"*After all*, what can we *ever* **gain** in **forever looking back** and **blaming ourselves** if our **lives** have *not turned out quite* as **we might have wished?**"

~ KAZUO ISHIGURO

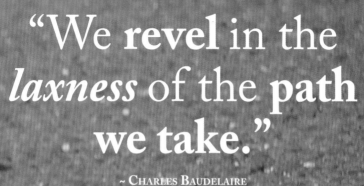

"We **revel** in the *laxness* of the **path** we take."

~ Charles Baudelaire

"*The* **most important thing** is to *enjoy* **your life**—to be **happy**— it's *all* that **matters.**"

~ AUDREY HEPBURN

"*Don't* be **betrayed** by **your laziness** to make you *think* there is **nothing** **you can do.**"

~ Kyos Magupe

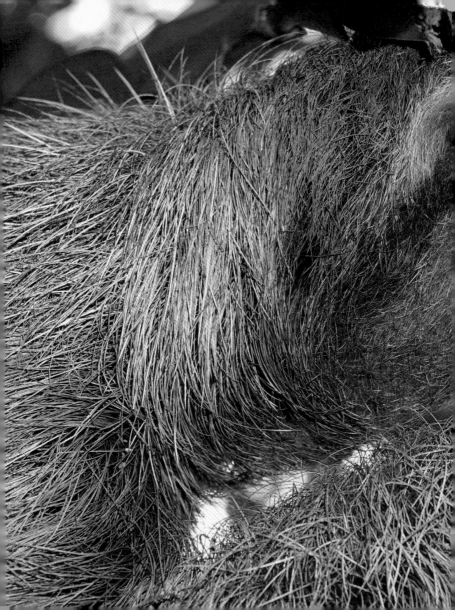

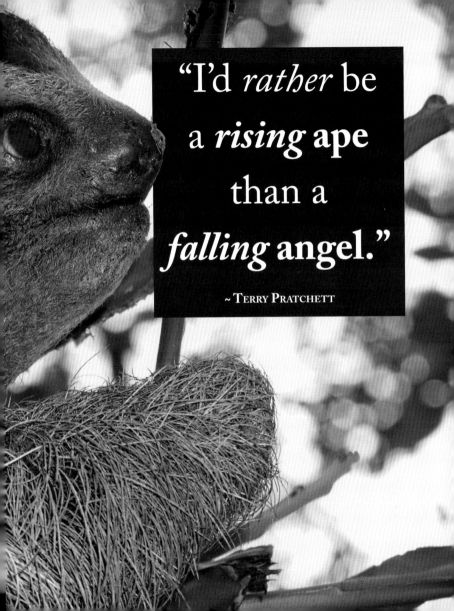

"I'd *rather* be a *rising* ape than a *falling* angel."

~ TERRY PRATCHETT

"*Whatever* you are, be a *good* **one.**"

~ Abraham Lincoln

"Laziness is *nothing* more than the **habit of resting** *before* you **get tired."**

~ Jules Renard

"Be *who* you are and say *what* you feel, because those who *mind* don't matter, and those who *matter* don't mind."

~ BERNARD M. BARUCH

"Honestly, if *you* were any **slower,** you'd be **going backward.**"

~ J. K. ROWLING

"People *say* **nothing** is **impossible,** but *I* do *nothing* every day."

~ A. A. Milne

"Your **children**
are not *your*
children. *They*
are the **sons and**
daughters of
Life's longing
for *itself.*"

~ KAHLIL GIBRAN

"The **bamboo** that *bends* is **stronger** than the **oak** that *resists*."

~ JAPANESE PROVERB

"Have no *fear* of **perfection**— you'll *never* reach it."

~ SALVADOR DALÍ

"To *see* the **hidden,**

you **hide** *yourself* too!"

~ Mehmet Murat ildan

"I've *heard* that **hard work** never *killed* anyone, but I say *why* take the **chance?**"

~ RONALD REAGAN

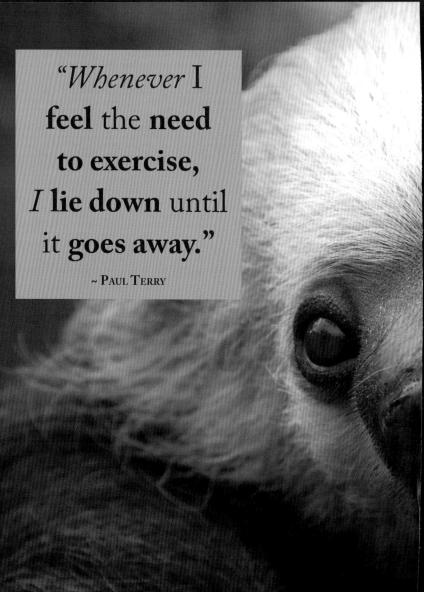

"*Whenever* I
feel the **need**
to **exercise**,
I **lie down** until
it **goes away.**"

~ Paul Terry

"*Every* great **dream** begins with a **dreamer.** *Always* **remember,** you have **within you** the **strength,** the **patience,** and the **passion** to *reach for the stars* to **change the world."**

~ HARRIET TUBMAN

"When engaged in **eating**, the *brain* should be the **servant** of the *stomach.*"

~ AGATHA CHRISTIE

"I **love** eating. I mean, I *really* *really* love **eating**."

~ MARTIN FREEMAN

"Time is an *illusion*. Lunchtime doubly so."

~ Douglas Adams

"**Failure** *concentrates* the **mind** *wonderfully.* *If* you **don't make mistakes,** you're *not* **trying hard enough.**"

~ JASPER FFORDE

"I'm always *trying* to **turn things upside down** and see *if they look* **any better.**"

~ Tibor Kalman

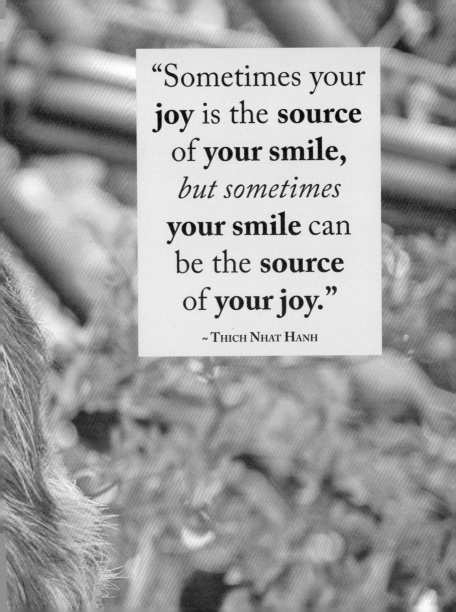

"Sometimes your **joy** is the **source** of **your smile,** *but sometimes* **your smile** can be the **source** of **your joy.**"

~ THICH NHAT HANH

"He devoted a considerable amount of his acute

intelligence to the cause of doing as little as possible."

~ James Herriot

"*Both* **teachers** and **learners** go to **sleep** at **their post** as *soon* as there is **no enemy** in the **field.**"

~ JOHN STUART MILL

"**You** have *your* **way. I** have *my* **way.** As for the *right* **way,** the *correct* **way, and** the *only* **way,** it *does not* **exist.**"

~ FRIEDRICH NIETZSCHE

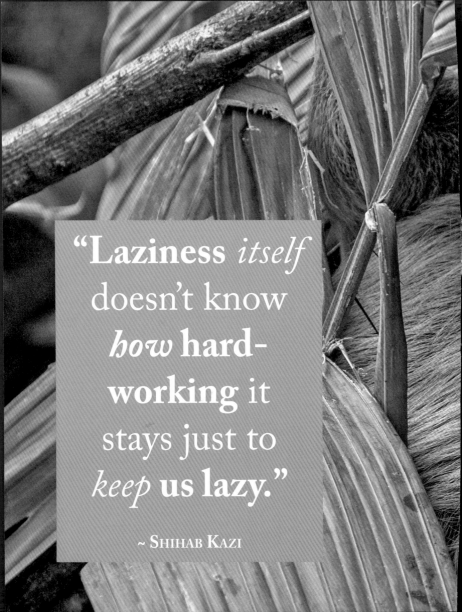

"Laziness *itself* doesn't know *how* hard-working it stays just to *keep* us lazy."

~ SHIHAB KAZI

too **old** and **wise**

. . . no, *not* too **old** and

silly for fairyland."

~ L. M. Montgomery

"For a **moment**, *nothing* happened. Then, after a **second or so**, nothing *continued* to happen."

~ Douglas Adams

"I am *not* **eccentric.**

It's **just** that

I am *more* **alive**

than *most* **people.** "

~ EDITH SITWELL

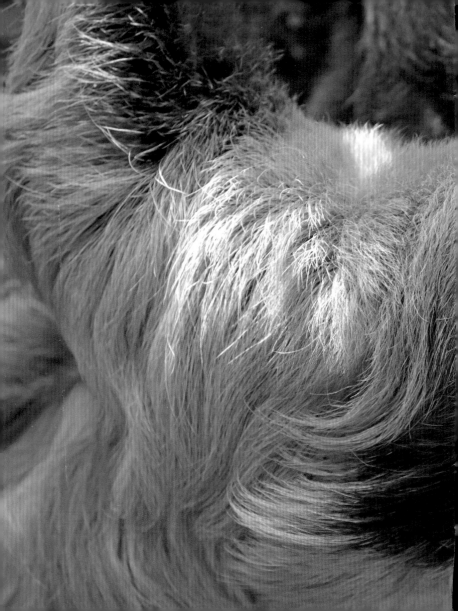

"In order to be **irreplaceable,** one *must always* be **different.**"

~ Coco Chanel

"Don't let's ever grow

"The *most* important kind of **freedom** is to be what you *really* are."

~ JIM MORRISON

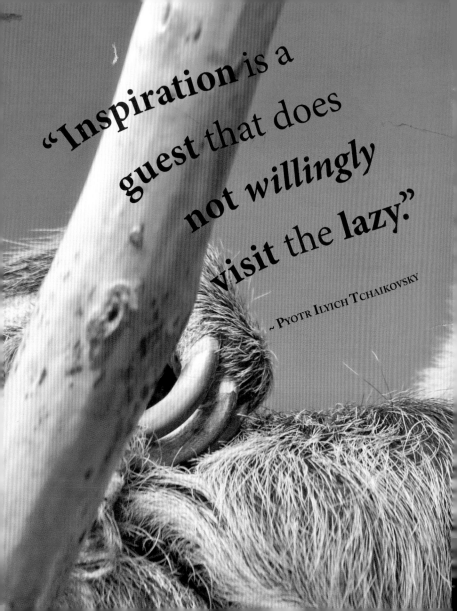

"Inspiration is a guest that does not willingly visit the lazy."

~ Pyotr Ilyich Tchaikovsky

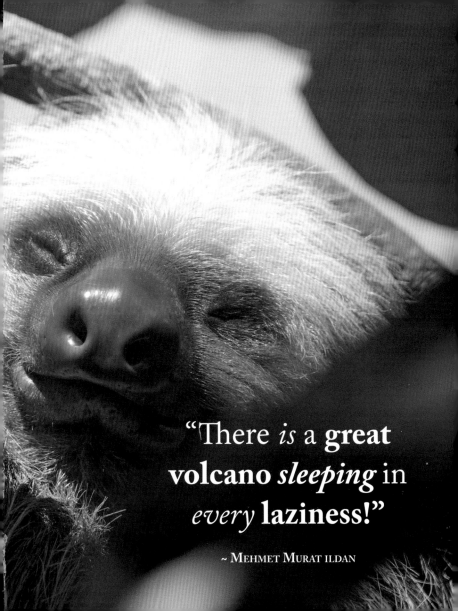

"There *is* a **great volcano** *sleeping* in *every* **laziness!**"

~ Mehmet Murat ildan

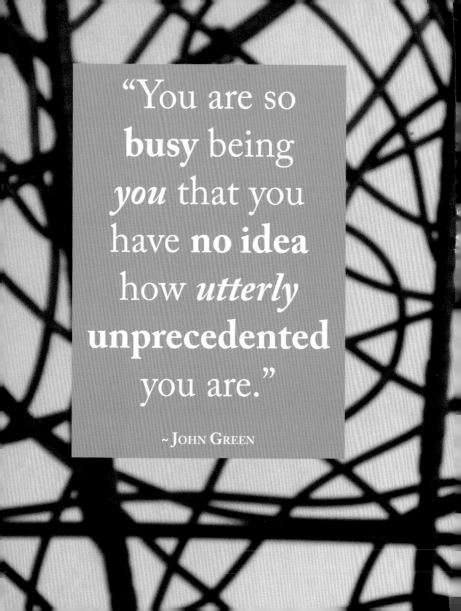

"You are so **busy** being *you* that you have **no idea** how *utterly* **unprecedented** you are."

~ JOHN GREEN

PICTURE CREDITS

"*Never* put off
till tomorrow
what *may* be
done the **day**
after **tomorrow**
just as well."

~ Mark Twain

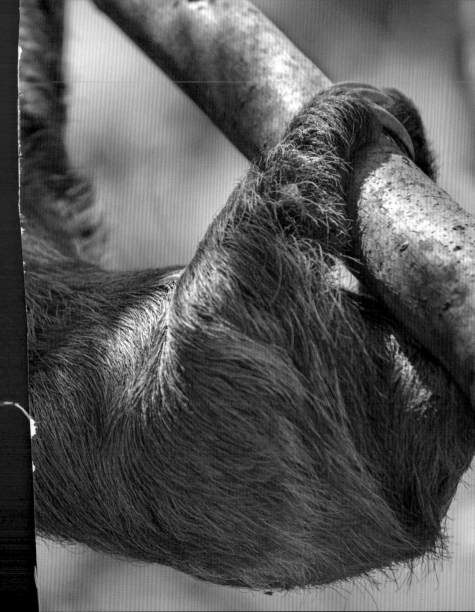

"Tomorrow
I'll *start*
thinking about
the day *after*
tomorrow. . . .
Maybe I *could*
do it **then;** but
not **today** . . ."

~ Fernando Pessoa

"**Progress** *isn't* made by **early risers.** It's made by **lazy men** *trying* to find **easier** ways to **do** *something.*"

~ Robert A. Heinlein

she is fierce."

~ William Shakespeare

"Though she be but little,